My Family Tree

ISBN 1 84298 088 2

Designed by
ANDREW MILNE DESIGN

Write to John Hunt Publishing Ltd
46a West Street, Alresford, Hampshire SO24 9AU, UK

A CIP catalogue record for this book is available from the British Library.

CARE for Education produces educational resources for nursery, primary and
secondary schools, gives guidance and training for teachers and school
governors/board members; facilitates conferences and seminars, and works on
educational policy with Government, local authorities, schools and parents.
Practice and policy work focuses on areas such as early years, school exclusion,
sex and relationships education and school management.

These Early Years books are part of the **Celebrating Marriage** resources
launched in 2001/2. More details of these resources can be found on the
website: www.celebratingmarriage.com

Printed in China

My Family Tree

Jacqueline Harding

Illustrated by
Margaret Brampton

John Hunt
Publishing Limited

My name is Sam.

My family and I have just moved into a new flat.

Here is my bedroom. It's small but I should get everything in here!

Come and look under my bed. When I unpacked I found lots of photos.

Here are photos of me as a baby!

Some photos are very old and some are torn.

Mum says I could make a Family Tree with them. A Family Tree shows who is in your family.

Look at this picture of me! Just above my picture are photos of my mum and dad.

Here is a picture of my grandma and grandad.

They are my mum's mum and dad.

I am their grandchild and dad says I laugh just like my grandad!

Here are photos of my dad's mum and dad.

They are also my grandparents and I am their grandchild too.

I have two grandmothers but I only have one grandfather because my other grandfather died when I was a baby.

Look at my great-grandmother!

My great-grandmother is my mother's mother. Dad says I smile like her!

This photo is my mother's sister, she is my aunt Jade.

Just below her photo are photos of her children. These children are my cousins.

Here is a photo of one of my cousins called Jo.

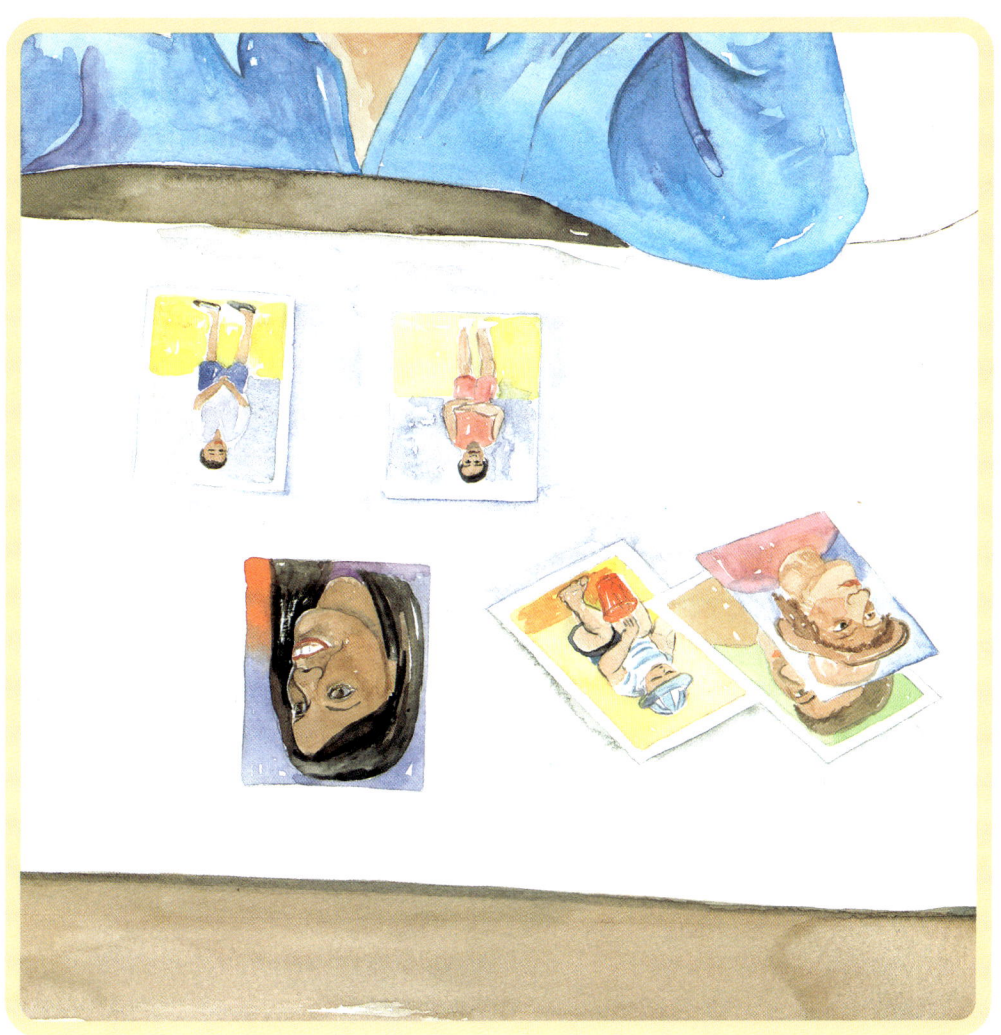

I couldn't find a photo of my grandmother's sister. So, I've drawn a picture of her. She likes playing the piano and has long fingers just like mine!

Mum is calling me. She says families help each other and I have to help with the unpacking!

This book can be read with children either individually or in groups. Invite the children to think about their Family Tree. Do they know who is in their family? (Children might use different names for their grandparents, for example, grandma, nanny or nana.)

Do they have and brothers or sisters?

Do they have any aunts or uncles?

Do the children think they look like any of their family?

It is important to be sensitive to different family structures and to emphasise that, however their family is made up, they can be sure that they are special.

You could bring your family photos for the children to see. Many young children will have been bridesmaids or pageboys or attended a wedding, so, if you are married you could show your wedding photos and talk about getting married. It will be essential to be sensitive to those children whose parents are not married or who have experienced divorce.

Young children love to talk about their families and will often ask for the same information to be given time and time again. It is as if they need to hear the story time after time in order to find their place within the family. They are fascinated by relationships and will try very hard to understand about cousins, aunts and uncles and their place within the relationship. A picture of a Family Tree might help their understanding.